50

fantastic ideas for
imaginative thinking

MARIANNE SARGENT

Published 2013 by Featherstone Education
Bloomsbury Publishing plc
50 Bedford Square, London, WC1B 3DP
www.bloomsbury.com

ISBN 978-1-4729-0846-9

Printed and bound in India by Replika Press Pvt. Ltd

This book is produced using paper that is made from wood grown in
managed, sustainable forests. It is natural, renewable and recyclable.
The logging and manufacturing processes conform to the environmental
regulations of the country of origin.

10 9 8 7 6 5 4 3 2 1

To see our full range of titles visit **www.bloomsbury.com**

Acknowledgements
Photographs with kind permission of London Early Years Foundation/
Emli Bendixen, and Acorn Childcare Ltd.

This book was inspired by the late Ros Bayley and her passionate quest to fire the
imaginations of both children and early years practitioners alike.

Contents

Introduction

In the wake of the influential *Effective Provision of Pre-school Education* research[1], there has been an increasing focus on helping young children to develop thinking skills. The previous *Statutory Framework for the Early Years Foundation Stage* emphasised the importance of involving children in sustained shared thinking by planning open-ended activities that foster discussion and debate[2]; the revised Early Years Foundation Stage has taken this a step further by identifying 'creating and thinking critically' as a key characteristic of effective learning. Early years practitioners are expected to plan opportunities for active exploration and play that lead to the use of creative and critical thinking skills.[3]

The newly structured curriculum further identifies communication and language as a prime area of learning and development. Much emphasis is placed upon the importance of helping children to improve the listening and attention skills that they need to be able to absorb and process information. Speaking skills are also now given due prominence, with an identified need for encouraging children to express themselves, as well as to ask and answer questions.

Furthermore, the new specific area, expressive arts and design, places emphasis on getting children to imagine, make-believe and create. This includes imaginative play, introducing storylines and narratives into play and representing ideas, thoughts and feelings in a variety of ways.

The aim of this book is to support practitioners as they strive to meet these expectations. It provides 50 suggestions for provocations and challenges that aim to fire children's imaginations, get them communicating with each other and using a broad range of creative and critical thinking skills.

[1] Siraj-Blatchford I, Sylva K, Melhuish E, Sammons P and Taggart (2004) *Effective Provision of Pre-school Education [EPPE]: Final Report*. Institute of Education, University of London.

[2] Department for Children, Schools and Families (DCSF) (2008) *Statutory Framework for the Early Years Foundation Stage*. (Revised edition) Nottingham, DCSF Publications

[3] Department for Education (DfE) (2012) *The Statutory Framework for the Early Years Foundation Stage*. Nottingham, DfE Publications.

There are different types of thinking and each encompasses various skills. None are exclusive and many overlap:

Enquiry: questioning, exploring, investigating, gathering information, looking at details.

Information processing: questioning, using information, organising, making connections, predicting, drawing upon own knowledge.

Reasoning: using logic, verbalising thoughts, planning, empathising, making links, predicting, speculating, explaining.

Problem-solving: forming strategies, weighing up, finding solutions, testing theories.

Evaluation: reflecting, recalling, judging, forming opinions, decision making, drawing conclusions.

Creative: forming ideas, fantasising, creating, looking for alternatives, designing, inventing, imagining, experimenting.

The provocations in this book aim to get children using all of these thinking skills at one time or another. There are three types of provocation:

★ **Fantastical provocations**: These take inspiration from fairy tales and fantasy and ask children to suspend their disbelief, engage in imaginative play and come up with explanations.

✔ **Problem-solving provocations**: These present a problem and ask the children to process information, weigh up a situation, generate ideas and make decisions.

♥ **Sensory provocations**: These appeal to the senses and aim to provoke an artistically creative response. Children are encouraged to explore phenomena and respond through art, music, dance and play.

The role of the practitioner

Most of the provocations in this book involve the practitioner setting them up and then taking a step back to observe the children's reactions. Practitioners should ask questions to generate discussion and debate, and use their observations to identify which direction the children are moving in. It is then possible to add stimulus and supply any resources that the children might need in order to extend their activities and explorations.

However, some of the provocations in the book are intended to be adult-led. They involve the practitioner presenting the children with something and facilitating a discussion about it. Specifically chosen resources are set out that help to guide the children in their investigations.

Although each provocation has a list of ideas for 'taking it further', practitioners will find that in most cases the children will take the provocation and run with it in all kinds of unexpected directions. This is what makes working this way so interesting and exciting.

Food allergy alert

When using food stuffs to enhance your play opportunties, always be mindful of potential food allergies. We have used this symbol on the relevant pages.

FOOD allergy !

Skin allergy alert

Some detergents and soaps can cause skin reactions. Always be mindful of potential skin allergies when letting children mix anything with their hands and always provide facilities to wash materials off after they have been in contact with the skin. Watch out for this symbol on the relevant pages.

SKIN allergy !

Safety issues

Social development can only take place when children can experiment and take reasonable risks in a safe environment. Encouraging independence, and the use of natural resources inevitably raises some health and safety issues, and where appropriate, these are identified with each activity.

Children need help and good models for washing their hands when using natural materials or preparing food. They may need reminding not to put things in their mouths, and to be careful with real-life or found resources.

SAFETY FIRST!

Buried treasure

★ Fantastical provocation

What you need:

- Shoe box
- Gold paint
- Gold marker pen
- Sticky back plastic
- Fake gems, jewellery and gold coins

What to do:

1. Paint a shoe box gold and draw patterns all over it with a marker pen to make it look like a treasure chest.

2. Cover the box in sticky back plastic to make it damp resistant.

3. Fill the box with fake treasure.

4. Bury the treasure chest in the sand pit or tray for the children to discover.

Question ideas:

★ Where do you think the treasure chest came from?

★ Why do you think they buried it here?

★ What do you think we should do with it?

★ What do think will happen if we …?

Taking it forward

- Write a letter from pirates asking if anyone has discovered their treasure. Seal the letter in a bottle and put it in the water tray. When the children discover it, read it out to them. Ask the children for ideas about what they should do next.

- Invite a volunteer to visit the setting dressed as a pirate and see what the children do. Encourage the children to question the pirate.

- Help the children to make their own treasure chests and create maps that lead to them.

What's in it for the children?

This provocation aims to get children fantasising and speculating.

Story suggestions

The Pirates Next Door and *The Pirate Cruncher* by Jonny Duddle (Templar Publishing)

Class Three All At Sea by Julia Jarman and Lynne Chapman (Hodder Children's Books)

Jolly Roger by Colin McNaughton (Walker)

The Night Pirates by Peter Harris and Deborah Allwright (Egmont)

Lost
✔ Problem-solving provocation

What you need:

- **Cuddly toy character or large puppet** (that the children will not recognise)
- **Small suitcase containing some belongings**
- **Piece of notepaper with 'Help!' written on it**

What to do:

1. Dress a puppet or cuddly toy character in a coat and stuff a note reading 'Help!' under its arm. (You could write the note in a different language.)
2. Fill a suitcase with the toy character's belongings.
3. Ask a volunteer to place the character on the outside of a door into the setting and knock.
4. Give the volunteer a moment to hide and send a child to answer the door.

Question ideas

★ Where do you think s/he is from?

★ Why do you think s/he is here?

★ What do you think happened?

★ How do you think s/he got here?

★ How do you think s/he is feeling?

★ What do you think we should do?

Taking it forward

- Ask the children what they can do to make the character feel at home. Help them find the resources they need to do so.
- Send the character home with different children at the weekend. Provide a diary and digital camera for the children to record what they get up to.
- Have a 'private investigator' visit the setting looking for the lost character. Send a letter to the toy's relatives to let them know s/he is all right.

What's in it for the children?

This provocation encourages children to empathise with others and think of ways to help.

Story suggestions

Paddington by Michael Bond, illustrated by R. W. Alley (HarperCollins)

Lost and Found by Oliver Jeffers (HarperCollins)

Sailor Bear by Martin Waddell and Virginia Austin (Walker)

One Bear Lost by Karen Hayles and Jenny Jones (Parragon)

Out of this world

★ Fantastical provocation

What you need:

- Cardboard boxes and junk for modelling
- Newspaper
- Fungicide–free cellulose paste
- Poster paint
- Marker pens
- PVA glue
- Outdoor rope light (optional)
- Soap flakes
- Food colouring

SKIN allergy!

Taking it forward

- Go on an alien hunt.
- After a few days, hide a toy alien in the outdoor area for the children to discover.
- Build a new spaceship for the alien to return home.
- Make a role-play spacecraft for the children to travel out into space.

What's in it for the children?

This provocation prompts the children to develop explanations and consider what might happen next.

Story suggestions

Q Pootle 5 by Nick Butterworth (HarperCollins)

Aliens in Underpants Save the World by Claire Freedman and Ben Cort (Simon & Schuster)

The Way Back Home by Oliver Jeffers (HarperCollins)

What to do:

1. There are two options for setting up this provocation.

   Either: Make a small spaceship using junk and cardboard, big enough for a toy alien. Cover it in papier mâché, paint it and draw on details to make it look convincing!

   Or: Make a life-size spaceship, using large cardboard boxes and drapes, which is big enough for a child to enter. Furnish the inside with alien possessions and control panels with buttons and switches. Light it up using an outdoor rope light.

2. Paint your spacecraft in watered-down PVA glue to make it more durable.

3. Put the spaceship in the outdoor area. Make it look as though it has crash-landed.

4. Make some 'slime' using soap flakes mixed with water and food colouring. Drip the 'slime' by nearby bushes or a wall to make it look as if something has run away!

Question ideas:

- What do you think this is?
- Where do you think it came from?
- Why do you think it is here?
- What do you think left the slime behind?
- Where do you think it went?

Silhouettes
♥ Sensory provocation

What you need:

- Large ironed white sheet
- Bright lamp

Or

- Overhead projector
- Projector screen or blank white wall
- Black paper
- Stencils
- Variety of everyday objects
- Pencil
- Scissors

Taking it forward

- Allow the children time to experiment with creating their own silhouettes. Provide torches for the children to experiment with.

- Hang a white sheet outside on a sunny day for the children to make shadows using the sun.

- Provide black sugar paper, stencils, pencils and scissors for the children to draw and cut out shapes.

What's in it for the children?

This provocation prompts children to investigate how something is created before attempting to recreate it themselves.

Story suggestions

Black on White and *White on Black*, both by Tana Hoban (William Morrow)

Jack's Amazing Shadow by Tom Percival (Pavilion)

What to do:

1. There are two options for setting up this provocation.

Either: Hang a large white sheet and shine a bright lamp on the sheet from behind.

Or: Set up an overhead projector and shine it on a blank white wall or screen.

2. Create a variety of silhouettes and ask the children to guess what object each silhouette represents.

Either: Use real objects and hold them up in between the light and the sheet to produce a silhouette that the children can see on the other side.

Or: Use stencils to draw out a variety of shapes on pieces of black paper. Cut each shape out and place the pieces of paper on an overhead projector to produce silhouettes that the children can see on a screen or wall.

Question ideas:

★ How do you think the silhouette is created?

★ Can you describe what you see?

★ What do you think the object is?

★ Can you create a silhouette?

➕ **Health & Safety**

Take care to ensure the children don't burn their hands on hot lamps and bulbs.

Where is it?

✔ Problem-solving provocation

What you need:

- Digital camera
- Laptop and projector

Taking it forward

■ Create a digital interactive map of the local area use PowerPoint or alternative presentation software:

1. Find a map of the local area on Google Maps and use it to create a title slide.

2. Create further slides that correspond with the locations you want to identify on the map. Label the slides according to the locations each will feature and insert your photographs.

3. Go back to the title slide featuring the map of the local area. Identify where each location is on the map and label it with a text box.

4. Create hyperlinks between the labels on the map and the corresponding slides featuring the locations.

5. Insert a 'back' button on each location slide with a hyperlink that returns to the map.

■ Allow the children to navigate the digital map.

■ Take them on a walk around the local area to visit the locations.

What's in it for the children?

This provocation involves children drawing on their own knowledge and memories, looking closely at details, making links and drawing conclusions.

What to do:

1. Walk around the local area and look for places that the children will be familiar with. For example:

   - playground
   - local park
   - leisure centre
   - shops
   - local medical practice.

2. Take a series of photographs that reveal clues about each location: some close-ups of individual items and features, some taken from strange angles and one that gives an overview of the whole place.

3. Bring the children together to show them the photographs and ask them if they can figure out where each location is.

4. After the children have made their guesses show them the final photograph revealing the identity of the location.

Question ideas:

★ What can you see?

★ Do you recognise anything in this photograph?

★ Where do you think you might find one of these?

★ Is this somewhere that you visit? How often? Who with? Why?

Story suggestions

Read books that encourage children to look for details, including:

Little Red Train: Busy Day by Benedict Blathwayt (Red Fox)

Each Peach Pear Plum or *Peepo*, both by Janet and Allan Ahlberg (Puffin)

Whose nest?

★ Fantastical provocation

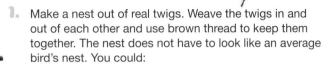

What you need:

- Twigs
- Brown thread

Taking it forward

- Put some golden eggs in the nest.
- Carry out surveillance of the nest. Do this by aiming a time-lapse camera focused on it:

  1. Set the camera to take a photo once every half hour over a weekend.

  2. In the meantime, take a series of photos from the same angle showing a creature approaching the nest and settling in it for a while.

  3. Upload the photos to an animation program such as Windows Movie Maker or iMovie and play it back to the children.

What's in it for the children?

This provocation asks children to draw on their own knowledge and experience to generate ideas.

··

Story suggestions

The Cow that Laid an Egg by Andy Cutbill and Russell Ayto (HarperCollins)

The Egg by M. P. Robertson (Frances Lincoln)

The Somethingosaur by Tony Mitton and Russell Ayto (HarperCollins)

The Odd Egg by Emily Gravett (Macmillan)

··

What to do:

1. Make a nest out of real twigs. Weave the twigs in and out of each other and use brown thread to keep them together. The nest does not have to look like an average bird's nest. You could:

   - make the nest any size you like – tiny, small, large or massive
   - try using unusual materials to make it – woven fabric, plastic straws, mud or clay
   - spray paint it a bright colour or cover it in glitter.

2. Put the nest somewhere in the outdoor area for the children to discover.

Question ideas:

★ What do you think built this nest?

★ What kind of creature would live in a nest like this?

★ Where do you think the creature is now?

★ Do you think it is going to come back? If so, when?

★ If you were to build a nest, what would you use and what would it look like?

Making music
♥ Sensory provocation

What you need:

- Selection of real musical instruments
- Everyday objects that can be used to make music: pots and pans; wooden, plastic and metal spoons; wooden blocks; bunches of keys; terracotta plant pots
- Plank of wood
- Glass bottles in various sizes and shapes
- Super glue
- Large box of materials for making instruments: plastic bottles and cups, yoghurt pots, toilet rolls, corrugated plastic and card, plastic plant pots, ribbons
- Masking tape
- Paper
- Elastic bands
- Computer
- Computer music program such as Mini Musical Monsters (Q&D Multimedia)
- CD/MP3 player
- Selection of CDs
- Sound station and microphones (TTS)

What to do:

1. Transform the setting into a music studio:
   - Set out a selection of real musical instruments.
   - Stick some glass bottles to a plank of wood with super glue. Fill the bottles with water to different levels.
   - Provide craft materials for the children to make their own instruments, including a large tub of cardboard tubes and boxes, and containers of beans, buttons and beads.
   - Install a music program on the setting computer.
   - Set up a CD player with a selection of CDs.
   - Provide a sound station with microphones.
2. Allow the children time and space to explore the resources and create.

Question ideas:

★ What does that sound like?
★ What do you like about that sound?
★ Can you sing that higher/lower?
★ Can you make a louder/quieter sound?
★ What can you hear?
★ What type of instrument are you making?
★ What are you going to use that for?
★ How does that work?
★ Can you clap in time to the music?

Health & Safety

Avoid broken glass by encouraging the children to blow across the tops of the bottles or otherwise closely supervising them if they are tapping the bottles.

Taking it forward

- Observe the children to find out what they most enjoying using.

- Challenge the children to invent and make their own instruments.

- Invite the children to bring instruments and resources from home.

- Invite parents in to spend time making music with their children

- Invite a group of musicians into the setting to play for the children..

What's in it for the children?

This provocation promotes creative musical expression and encourages children to invent and design instruments of their own.

> **Story suggestions**
>
> *I am the Music Man* by Debra Potter (Child's Play)
>
> *Geraldine the Music Mouse* by Leo Lionni (Dragonfly Books)
>
> *The Animal Boogie* (with CD) by Debbie Harter (Barefoot Books)

A load of rubbish

✔ Problem-solving provocation

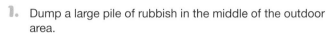

What you need:

- **Information book about rubbish and recycling** (such as *Rubbish and Recycling* by Alex Frith and Peter Allen (Usborne))

- **Large amount of clean rubbish: plastic tubs and bottles, paper, cardboard packaging, metal cans** (without any sharp edges), **old fabrics and broken electrical items**

Taking it forward

- Set up a role-play household waste-sorting site.

- Ask the children for suggestions for how to reuse some of the rubbish. Can they find any uses? Do they have any craft ideas?

- Help the children to sort the rubbish for correct disposal.

What's in it for the children?

This provocation involves children gathering information and using what they learn to plan and execute a project.

> **Story suggestions**
>
> *George Saves the World by Lunchtime* by Jo Readman and Ley Honor Roberts (Eden Children's Books)
>
> *The Adventures of a Plastic Bottle: A Story About Recycling* by Alison Inches and Pete Whitehead (Little Simon)
>
> *Litterbug Doug* by Ellie Bethel (Meadowside Children's Books)

What to do:

1. Dump a large pile of rubbish in the middle of the outdoor area.

2. Wait until the children arrive and exclaim that you have had a visit from fly tippers in the night.

3. Explain what fly tipping is and ask the children what they think the culprit should have done with the rubbish.

4. Ask the children what they can do to solve the problem. Use an information book to help facilitate discussion.

Question ideas:

★ What do you think has happened here?

★ Who do you think left all this rubbish?

★ What should have been done with the rubbish?

★ What do you think we should do next?

Fanciful fruit
♥ Sensory provocation

What you need:

- Large plant pots
- Small leafy branches from different types of tree
- Coloured and metallic spray paints
- Soil or sand
- Selection of strong-smelling spices: cinnamon, curry powder, five spice, ginger, cloves, nutmeg, cumin

FOOD allergy!

Taking it forward

- Provide art materials for the children to draw, paint pictures and make dough models of their fanciful fruits.
- Examine a selection of exotic fruits, cut them open, smell and taste them.
- Plant fruit seeds and grow fruit trees.

What's in it for the children?

This provocation uses the children's sense of smell to provoke an imaginative and inventive response.

> Story suggestions
>
> *Oliver's Fruit Salad* by Vivian French and Alison Bartlett (Hodder Children's Books)
>
> *Fruits* by Valerie Bloom and David Axtell (Macmillan)
>
> *The Giving Tree* by Shel Silverstein (Particular Books)

What to do:

1. Collect some small leafy tree branches from different types of tree.
2. Spray paint the branches and leaves different colours.
3. Plant the branches in large pots filled with sand or soil so that they look like small trees.
4. Sprinkle some strong-smelling spices around the base of each tree on top of the soil.
5. Place the trees around the setting, a little apart from each other.
6. Explain to the children that these are magical trees that bear fanciful fruits. Allow the children to take a closer look at the trees and smell the scents coming from them.
7. Ask the children if they can imagine what the fruit might look and taste like.

Question ideas:

- ★ Can you describe that smell?
- ★ What kind of fruit do you think would grow on a tree that smells like that?
- ★ What shape do you think the fruit might be?
- ★ What colour do you think the fruit might be?
- ★ What do you think the seed for this tree might look like?

Crime scene

✔ Problem-solving provocation

What you need:

- **Police cordon tape** (available from www.suecowley.co.uk)
- **'Crime Scene' sign**
- **Shoes with deep treads**
- **Mud**
- **Pencil and paper**

Taking it forward

- Ask someone to wait on standby at the end of the phone so the children can call the 'police' and report the crime.
- Set up a police incident room with role-play investigation equipment, including clipboards, notepads, pencils, magnifiers, dictaphones, digital cameras and tape measures.
- Invite the police into the setting. Help the children prepare for the visit by collating their evidence ready to present it.

What's in it for the children?

This provocation asks children to make observations, gather evidence, process information and draw conclusions.

Story suggestions

Burglar Bill by Allan and Janet Ahlberg (Puffin)

Shifty McGifty and Slippery Sam by Tracey Corderoy and Steven Lenton (Nosy Crow)

Who Pushed Humpty Dumpty? And Other Notorious Nursery Tale Mysteries by David Levinthal and John Nickle (Random House)

The Highway Rat by Julia Donaldson and Axel Scheffler (Alison Green Books)

What to do:

1. Cordon off an area of the setting and put up a sign saying 'Crime Scene'. You could use the role-play house or shop and make it look as though it has been broken into and burgled.

2. Make muddy footprints leading up to a window or door.

3. Create fingerprints by heavily shading a piece of paper with a pencil, pressing your fingers onto it and then transferring the prints to areas around the scene.

Question ideas:

★ What do you think has happened here?

★ What crime do you think has been committed?

★ What do you think we should do?

★ How do you think we could go about collecting the evidence?

★ How do you think we could collect samples of these fingerprints/footprints?

Lost property

★ Fantastical provocation

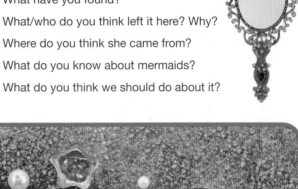

What you need:

- Purse decorated in seashells
- Pearl necklace
- Mother of pearl comb and mirror
- Large rock
- Water tray
- Sand

What to do:

1. Place the purse, necklace, comb and mirror on a large rock in the water tray and leave it there for the children to discover. If possible, do this using an extra large water tray outside.

2. Sprinkle a trace of sand in the bottom of the tray. You could even leave a trail of sand leading to a door, window, sink or outside drain.

Question ideas:

★ What have you found?

★ What/who do you think left it here? Why?

★ Where do you think she came from?

★ What do you know about mermaids?

★ What do you think we should do about it?

Taking it forward

- Find out more about mythical sea creatures.

- Hint at the idea that the items may carry magical powers. Ask the children to suggest what kind of powers.

What's in it for the children?

This provocation asks children to look at evidence, speculate and come up with imaginative explanations.

Story suggestions

Can You Catch a Mermaid? by Jane Ray (Orchard)

The Singing Mermaid by Julia Donaldson and Lydia Monks (Macmillan)

Baffling beads
♥ Sensory provocation

What you need:

- Selection of beads made from different materials and in a variety of colours, shapes and sizes
- String or laces
- Sorting bowls
- Large tray
- Scoops

What to do:

1. Put beads all over the setting:

   - Fill sorting bowls with beads and place them on tables.

   - Fill a large tray with beads and accompanying scoops.

   - Thread beads onto strings or laces. Arrange the beads randomly on some and in patterns on others. Lay them on the floors and tables. Wrap them around chairs. Hang them from the ceiling, off door handles and from high furniture.

Question ideas

★ Can you describe that pattern?

★ How many beads have you got?

★ Which is your favourite type of bead?

★ What kinds of things can you do with beads?

Taking it forward

- Help the children to copy bead patterns and create their own.

- Leave tubes of various lengths and sizes lying around and see what the children do with them.

- Take the children out on a nature walk to look for natural items that they can use as beads, for example, shells, conkers, pinecones and chestnuts. Ask them for ideas about how to make holes in the found objects. Show them the tools needed and demonstrate how to do this safely.

What's in it for the children?

This provocation aims to get children exploring and experimenting with size, shape, colour and pattern.

> **Story suggestions**
>
> *A String of Beads* by Margarette S. Reid and Ashley Wolff (E P Dutton & Co)

➕ **Health & Safety**

Remind the children to never put beads or natural items in their mouths.

I'm stuck!

✔ Problem-solving provocation

What you need:

- A popular and familiar cuddly toy or puppet from the setting

What to do:

1. Put a popular cuddly toy or puppet somewhere difficult to reach. This could be on a roof, up a tree, on top of a high fence or clinging to a drainpipe.

2. Wait for the children to notice it.

Question ideas

★ How do you think he got up there?

★ What do you think he was trying to do?

★ How do you think he is feeling?

★ What do you think we should do?

★ Would it be safe to do that? Why/why not?

Health & Safety

Ask for the caretaker or site manager's assistance when using high ladders.

Taking it forward

- Put the children in talk partners and ask them to consider:
  - What would have happened if the toy had been stranded somewhere else?
  - What would have happened if they had not discovered the toy?

What's in it for the children?

This provocation involves children discussing and evaluating ideas before deciding what to do next.

Story suggestions

Stuck by Oliver Jeffers (HarperCollins)

Stuck in the Mud by Garry Parsons and Jane Clarke (Puffin)

Book of Spells
★ Fantastical provocation

What you need:

- Large hardback book with plain pages
- Metallic pen
- Metallic star stickers
- Teabags
- Black pen
- Red pen
- Talcum powder

Question ideas

★ What do you think it is?

★ Who do you think wrote this book?

★ How do you think the book got there?

★ What do you think this spell will do?

What to do:

1. Make a large hardback book look magical. Stick stars on the cover and write a title such as 'Book of Spells' in a fancy font using a metallic pen.

2. Fill the book with imaginary spells.

3. Use a different coloured pen to cross out ingredients and change quantities. Add notes about how the spells worked or failed.

4. Age the book by ripping some of the pages, scuffing up the edges and creasing the spine and cover. Rub damp teabags over the pages to stain them.

5. Sprinkle talcum powder in between some of the pages to represent dust.

6. Leave the book in the reading corner for the children to discover.

Shrinking potion

Ingredients

1 eye of a newt

2 toad's legs

1 handful of pondweed

½ jug of warm water

15 grains of sand

Instructions

1. Squash the eye of a newt between your fingers and drop it into ½ jug of warm water.

2. Crush the toad's legs and drop them in, stirring in an anticlockwise direction.

3. Add the pondweed and continue to stir.

4. Drop in one grain of sand at a time, while stirring in a clockwise direction and uttering the words, 'Ippity, uppity, oppity, zink, make me a potion to make something shrink!'

Taking it forward

- Put a cauldron, jugs, large spoons and old pots and pans in the outdoor area for the children to make magical concoctions using natural ingredients such as mud, water, stones, flowers and grass.

- Invite the children to make up spells of their own.

- Challenge the children to make magic wands using anything they like, including craft and natural materials.

What's in it for the children?

This provocation presents the children with a make-believe mystery and asks them to invent a little magic of their own.

 Health & Safety

Take care to ensure the children do not actually consume the magical potions they concoct.

Story suggestions

Spells by Emily Gravett (Macmillan)

Meg's Cauldron based upon the books by Helen Nicoll and Jan Pieńkowski (Ladybird)

Winnie's Magic Wand by Valerie Thomas and Korky Paul (Oxford University Press)

Room on the Broom by Julia Donaldson and Axel Scheffler (Macmillan)

Hop on

★ Fantastical provocation

What you need:

- **Very large cardboard boxes**
- **Poster paint**
- **Black marker pen**
- **PVA glue**
- **Round tin foil serving plate**
- **Long cardboard tube**
- **Glitter**
- **Sticky tape**
- **An A-board** (or something to use as a sign)

Taking it forward

- Provide materials for the children to build their own magical vehicles.
- Help the children to retell the stories about their magical journeys and draw maps.

What's in it for the children?

This provocation supports children's excursions into the make-believe and encourages them to engage in imaginative play.

Story suggestions

The Flying Diggers by Ian Whybrow and David Melling (Hodder Children's Books)

The Wheels on the Bus Go Round and Round by Annie Kubler (Child's Play Ltd.)

The Hundred Decker Bus by Mike Smith (Macmillan)

What to do:

1. Make a bus out of some large cardboard boxes. Make it large enough for the children to sit inside.

2. Paint the bus and draw on details with a marker pen. Write 'Magical Bus Tours' across the side.

3. Give the bus a coat of watered down PVA glue mixed with glitter.

4. Make a steering wheel. Snip around one edge of a long cardboard tube and fold back the tabs. Sticky tape the tube to the base of a large round tinfoil serving plate. Make a hole in the front of the bus and feed the tube through. Decorate the steering wheel with glitter and sparkles to make it look as if it has magical qualities.

5. Put a sign up next to the bus saying 'Next tour leaves in 5 minutes'.

Question ideas

★ Where do you think the bus came from?

★ Where do you think the bus might go?

★ Where would you like the bus to take you?

★ Can you tell me about the last time you went on a bus?

Budge it

✔ Problem-solving provocation

What you need:

- Massive cardboard box
- Small items to fill the container
- Packing tape
- Address label

What to do:

1. Fill a massive cardboard box with small items. The box should be heavy enough that the children are unable to move it without help.

2. Tape up the box and stick an address label on it.

3. Place the box in front of an entrance that the children frequently use, or else in an inconvenient place.

4. Explain that the box was delivered early this morning and unfortunately the delivery person has left it in a very inconvenient spot.

5. Explain that the box is too heavy to move and ask the children if they have any suggestions about what you can do.

Question ideas

★ Why do you think the box is so heavy?

★ What might be inside?

★ Do you have any ideas about how we can move it?

★ What equipment do you need to help with that?

Taking it forward

- Provide wheelbarrows and trailers for children to move things around in the outdoor area.

- Provide buckets and ropes for the children to create pulleys for lifting.

- Bring the children together to talk about lifting things safely and taking care of their muscles and backs.

What's in it for the children?

This provocation requires the children to communicate with each other and work as a team to solve a problem.

Story suggestions

Mr Strong by Roger Hargreaves (Egmont)

I Am So Strong by Mario Ramos (Gecko Press)

✚ Health & Safety

- Ensure the container is not blocking any entrance that serves as a fire exit.

- Take care to ensure that children do not strain themselves when attempting to move anything heavy.

Powerful package

★ Fantastical provocation

What you need:

- **Chest** (or large box painted and decorated to look like a chest)
- Large luggage label

  And

- Selection of superhero capes

  Or

- Sewing machine
- Pillow cases
- Ribbon
- Fabric pens

What to do:

1. Fill a large chest with superhero capes. To make capes, use pillowcases in various colours:
   - decorate them with fabric pens or use a sewing machine to embroider details
   - stitch a strip of fabric or ribbon across the top of each pillow case for tying the cape around shoulders.

2. Attach a large luggage label to the case with a message, such as:

   '*Open this chest and peek inside, a great many powers you will find.*'

3. Leave the chest in the middle of the setting for the children to discover.

Question ideas

★ Where do you think this came from?

★ What do you think these are?

★ Have you ever seen anything like this before?

★ What do you think that symbol means?

★ What do you think will happen if you put one of the capes on?

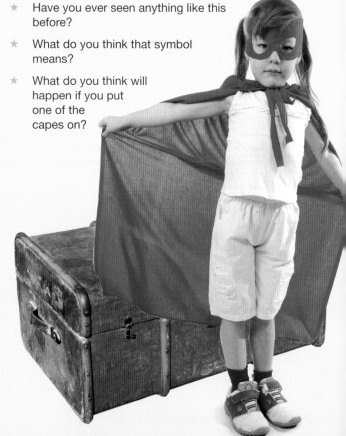

Taking it forward

- Challenge the children to invent their own superheroes:

  - ask them to give their hero a superpower and a name

  - help them to design a cape for their hero.

- Bring the children together to talk about the superheroes and villains in their favourite films/television programmes. Talk through the storylines, consider the actions of the characters and discuss the consequences of such behaviour in real life situations. Useful reference books on this subject are *Re-thinking Superhero and Weapon Play* by Steven Popper (Open University Press) and *We Don't Play with Guns Here* by Penny Holland (Open University Press).

What's in it for the children?

This provocation asks children to draw upon their knowledge and interest of superhero play and asks them to come up with inventive ideas.

Story suggestions

Superworm by Julia Donaldson and Axel Scheffler (Alison Green Books)

Elmer and Super El by David McKee (Andersen)

The King of Space by Jonny Duddle (Templar)

Charlie's Superhero Underpants by Paul Bright and Lee Wildish (Little Tiger Press)

The secret party

★ Fantastical provocation

What you need:

- Balloons, streamers, party poppers, party hats
- Paper plates and plastic cups
- Party food
- Party music CD
- Wrapping paper

What to do:

1. Make it look as though someone had a party in the setting overnight.

   - Throw some streamers and pop some party poppers.
   - Scatter a few balloons around, and pop some.
   - Leave some crumpled wrapping paper lying around.
   - Put out some drained plastic cups and paper plates containing half-eaten party food.
   - Put a party music CD in the sound system.

Question ideas

- ★ What on earth has been going on here?
- ★ Who do you think was here?
- ★ What do you think they were doing?
- ★ Why do you think they were having a party?
- ★ How do you think they got in?
- ★ Where do you think they are now?

Taking it forward

- Involve the children in organising their own party.

  - Help them make party hats and decorations, bake cakes and prepare food.
  - Help them make invitations for parents and siblings.

What's in it for the children?

This provocation aims to get children puzzling and asking questions.

Story suggestions

Kipper's Birthday by Mick Inkpen (Hodder Children's Books)

Spot Goes to a Party by Eric Hill (Puffin)

This is Actually My Party by Lauren Child (Puffin)

The Birthday Party by Helen Oxenbury (Walker)

Catch a falling star
♥ Sensory provocation

What you need:

- Laptop and projector
- Overhead projector
- Light box
- Card
- Tinfoil
- Stars made out of different materials: plastic, card, wood, fabric, metal and smooth glass
- Star-shaped Christmas lights
- Silver spray paint
- Star-shaped printing sponges and paints
- Star-shaped stencils
- Glow in the dark stars
- Cotton thread

Taking it forward

- Show the children images of real stars.
- Ask the children if there are any other shapes that they would like to decorate the setting with. Help them to create the shapes.

What's in it for the children?

This provocation aims to help the children make discoveries through exploration of a range of images, objects and materials.

Story suggestions

How to Catch a Star by Oliver Jeffers (HarperCollins)

Laura's Star by Klaus Baumgart (Little Tiger Press)

What to do:

1. Decorate the whole setting – indoors and outside – with stars:

   - Bury wooden stars in the sand tray.
   - Put colourful smooth glass stars in the water tray.
   - Cut out tin foil stars and stick them on the walls.
   - Attach stars to strings and hang them off fences and in trees.
   - Hang up star-shaped Christmas lights.
   - Spray paint silver stars on the floor of the outdoor area.
   - Project star shapes onto the walls and ceilings.
   - Put transparent plastic coloured stars on a light box.
   - Put out star-shaped stencils, sponges and paint.
   - Stick glow-in-the-dark stars to a ceiling in a room that is easily darkened.

Question ideas

★ What shape can you see everywhere?
★ Where else have you seen a star before?
★ Where do you think they came from?
★ Can you make/draw/paint a star?

Secret scrapbook
★ Fantastical provocation

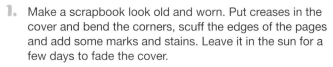

What you need:

- Scrapbook
- Glue
- Sticky tape
- Old postcards
- Old photographs
- Digital camera
- Writing paper
- Old travel and admission tickets
- Different coloured pens

Top tip ★

Find old postcards in charity shops and download old photographs from the internet.

Taking it forward

- Send home scrapbooks with the children and invite parents to help fill them with memorabilia.

What's in it for the children?

This provocation asks the children use information and details to make evidence-based assumptions.

Story suggestions

My Secret Scrapbook Diary: Little Red Riding Hood, Cinderella, Jack and the Beanstalk and *The Three Little Pigs,* all by Kees Moerbeek (Child's Play)

What to do:

1. Make a scrapbook look old and worn. Put creases in the cover and bend the corners, scuff the edges of the pages and add some marks and stains. Leave it in the sun for a few days to fade the cover.

2. Decide who owned the scrapbook: make up a fictional character and fill the scrapbook with their memorabilia.

   - Type and write letters using different pens. Age the paper by scrunching it up and wiping wet teabags over it.
   - Write old postcards as if they have been sent from friends.
   - Include old photographs and postcards from past holidays.
   - Take photographs of the area where the character comes from. Age the photographs using a program like Adobe Photoshop.
   - Stick in travel and admission tickets from places the character has visited.
   - Write labels, draw pictures and add doodles to the pages.

3. Hide the scrapbook somewhere in the setting where the children will discover it.

Question ideas

- ★ What do you think this is?
- ★ Who do you think put it together?
- ★ What does the scrapbook tell us about its owner?
- ★ How long do you think it has been there?

Broken down

✔ Problem-solving provocation

What you need:

- **Large toy character or puppet** (that the children will not recognise)

- **Ride-on car** (that the children will not recognise)

- **Washable black paint or shoe polish**

Taking it forward

- Provide role-play mechanic equipment for the children to use to fix the car.

- Help the children make a taxicab using cardboard boxes so that they can take the character wherever he wants to go.

What's in it for the children?

This provocation aims to get the children involved in a role-play scenario that entails coming up with helpful ideas.

Story suggestions

Duck in the Truck by Jez Alborough (HarperCollins)

Mr Grumpy's Motor Car by John Burningham (Red Fox)

What to do:

1. Dress a toy character or puppet and use some black paint or shoe polish to make black streaks on its face, arms and clothes.

2. Ask a volunteer to park the ride-on car somewhere safe just outside the setting. Make it look like the car has broken down or is stuck in some mud, a pothole or a ditch.

3. Ask the volunteer to place the toy character or puppet on the outside of a door into the setting and knock.

4. Give the volunteer time to hide and send a child to answer the door.

5. Use the character to draw the children's attention to the car parked just outside.

Question ideas

★ Why do you think he stopped here?

★ What do you think has happened?

★ Where do you think he might be from?

★ Where do you think he is going?

★ What do you think we can do to help?

★ Have you ever been in a broken down vehicle?

Ice castle
♥ Sensory provocation

What you need:

- Water
- Castle-shaped buckets
- Tubs and cups in various shapes and sizes
- Food colouring in various shades
- Glitter in various colours
- Fake gems (available from www.tts-group.co.uk)
- Spoon
- Large freezer
- Iced water
- Spray bottle
- Shallow tray with raised edges

What to do:

1. Fill up several castle-shaped buckets and various tubs and cups with water. Sprinkle some glitter and mix a few drops of food colouring into each container and stir.

2. Drop a handful of fake gems into one of the buckets.

3. Put the containers in a chest freezer over night.

4. First thing in the morning before the children arrive, remove the containers from the freezer, leave them out to loosen the ice and then tip out the shaped blocks.

5. Put the blocks of ice together to create a sculpture of a castle:
   - Place the blocks of ice inside a shallow tray with raised edges.
   - Use a water spray filled with iced water to stick them together.
   - Place the block containing the fake gems at the centre of the sculpture.

6. Leave the sculpture for the children to discover.

Question ideas

★ Who do you think created it?

★ How do you think they did it?

★ What do you think is in the middle?

★ How do you think we could get to it?

Taking it forward

- Provide torches with coloured bulbs and mirrors for the children to use while exploring the sculpture.

- Invite the children to give suggestions for ice sculptures that they would like to create. Help them choose containers, fill them with water and put them in them in the freezer.

- Make snow sculptures in freezing weather.

What's in it for the children?

This provocation involves hands-on investigation to discover how something is created.

Story suggestions

Here Comes Jack Frost by Kazuno Kohara (Square Fish)

The Tale of Jack Frost by David Melling (Hodder Children's Books)

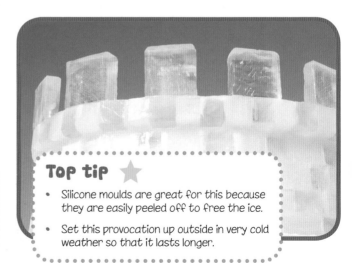

Top tip ★

- Silicone moulds are great for this because they are easily peeled off to free the ice.

- Set this provocation up outside in very cold weather so that it lasts longer.

Vacant vivarium

✔ Problem-solving provocation

What you need:

- Vivarium
- **Small plants** (plastic or real from a pet shop)
- Gravel
- Water bowl
- Rocks

Taking it forward

- Buy or borrow a pet to live inside the vivarium.

- Help the children make 'missing' posters in case someone spots the creature. Prompt them to include information and details, such as how big the creature might be and what type of animal inhabits such an enclosure.

What's in it for the children?

This provocation encourages children to gather information and use it to formulate theories and ideas.

Story suggestions

The Snake who Came to Stay by Julia Donaldson (Barrington Stoke)

Class Two at the Zoo by Julia Jarman and Lynne Chapman (Hodder Children's Books)

The Great Pet Sale by Mick Inkpen (Hodder Children's Books)

What to do:

1. Set up a vivarium to make it look as if a creature lives inside it:

- cover the base in gravel
- put in some small plants and rocks
- fill a water bowl.

2. Open the lid of the vivarium and leave it for the children to discover.

Question ideas

★ Who do you think the vivarium belongs to?

★ What do you think lives in it?

★ What kind of creature lives in a vivarium like this?

★ How big do you think the creature might be?

★ Where do you think the creature is?

★ How do you think it got out?

★ What do you think we should do?

The lonely robot

★ Fantastical provocation

What you need:

- Cardboard boxes
- Junk: cardboard tubes, plastic tubs, yoghurt pots, egg boxes
- Sticky tape
- Gold and silver paint
- Metallic shape stickers
- Black marker pens
- PVA glue
- White card

What to do:

1. Make a robot out of cardboard boxes and junk. The robot can be as large as you like. Paint it silver and gold, stick on metallic stickers and draw on details with a marker pen. Coat it in watered-down PVA glue to make it more durable.

2. Type out a message explaining that the robot is lonely because he has been separated from his friends and family. Cut a slit in the robot's belly and push in the message, leaving a bit sticking out.

3. Place the robot in the middle of the setting for the children to discover.

Question ideas

★ Where do you think he came from?

★ What do you think happened to his friends and family?

★ What do you think we can do to help him?

★ Who do you think typed that message?

Taking it forward

- Provide thin card and pens for the children to write messages to stick into the slot in the robot's belly.

- Help the children make robot friends for the visiting robot. Encourage them to think about the different functions they would like their robot to have:

  - Does their robot serve a purpose?

  - Do the buttons have functions?

  - Are the children able to create moving parts?

- Take the children to a large space where they can move like robots. Use large cardboard boxes to make costumes – cut holes in the sides for arms, in the bottom for legs and in the front for faces.

What's in it for the children?

This provocation aims to prompt children to come up with innovative and creative ideas.

Story suggestions

The Robot Book by Heather Brown (Accord Publishing)

Harry and the Robots by Ian Whybrow and Adrian Reynolds (Puffin)

No-Bot, the Robot with No Bottom! by Sue Hendra (Simon & Schuster)

Aeroplane arrivals

♥ Sensory provocation

What you need:

- Paper in a variety of different colours and sizes
- Cotton thread

What to do:

1. Make a large number of paper aeroplanes in different colours and sizes. Put them all over the setting:
   - hanging from the ceiling
   - on top of tall furniture and shelving
   - on tables and under chairs
   - in equipment drawers and resource containers
   - scattered all over the floor
   - stuck to windows.
2. When the children arrive, give them time and space to play with the paper aeroplanes.
3. Follow the children's lead and provide assistance and support for any investigations or activities they embark upon.

Question ideas

★ Where do you think these came from?

★ Do you know how to make a paper aeroplane?

★ What do you want to do with them?

★ What do you think would happen if…?

★ Why don't you try it and see?

Taking it forward

- Take the aeroplanes out into a wide-open space to throw. Find a hill to launch them from.
- Help the children make their own paper aeroplanes. Use templates from the internet or a book such as *100 Paper Planes to Fold and Fly* by Andy Tudor (Usborne).
- Encourage the children to design and test their own aeroplanes. Have a contest to see which aeroplane flies the furthest.

What's in it for the children?

This provocation aims to get children investigating how something works before creating and testing a design of their own.

> **Story suggestions**
>
> *Amazing Aeroplanes* by Tony Mitton and Ant Parker (Kingfisher)
>
> *Moon Plane* by Peter McCarty (Henry Holt & Company)

SOS!

✔ Problem-solving provocation

Help!

What you need:

- **Arrangements for an off-site visit: risk assessment, adequate adult to child ratios** (plan ahead without telling the children)
- **Adult volunteer**
- **Phone**
- **Relevant rescue equipment**

EMERGENCY

Taking it forward

- Ask the children to think about what you could have done (who you could have called) if you had been unable to rescue the stranded person.
- Arrange for a visit from the fire service, a local search and rescue service or the Royal National Lifeboat Institute. Ask them to bring in some of their equipment for the children to examine and try to work out what it is used for.

What's in it for the children?

This provocation aims to get children to evaluate a situation, weigh up risk, discuss solutions and try out ideas.

Story suggestions

The Rescue Party by Nick Butterworth (HarperCollins)

Albert Le Blanc to the Rescue by Nick Butterworth (HarperCollins)

What to do:

1. Set up an emergency situation. Use a local park or a place elsewhere on the setting premises. Ask an adult volunteer to get himself stranded somewhere, for example, up a tree, down a hole or locked in a cupboard. Ensure you have the relevant rescue equipment somewhere easily accessible!

2. Get the volunteer to phone the setting to alert everyone that they are in trouble.

3. Take the children in small groups to rescue the adult in trouble.

Question ideas

★ What do you think has happened?

★ How do you think he got there?

★ What do you think we need to do to rescue him?

★ What items do you think we need to be able to rescue him?

★ Where do you think we can find the things we need?

★ Is there anyone who you think might be able to help?

50 fantastic ideas for imaginative thinking

Puzzle by post

✔ Problem-solving provocation

What you need:

- Envelopes
- Large jigsaw puzzle
- Fake postage stamps

What to do:

1. Choose a large puzzle that links to a current topic. Otherwise choose any puzzle and write a cryptic message on the back that will be revealed when the puzzle is completed.

2. Take the puzzle apart and put each of the pieces in individual envelopes.

3. Write the setting's address on each of the envelopes, stick on fake postage stamps and draw on postmarks.

4. Set aside an area for constructing the puzzle over a period of weeks.

5. Have someone deliver one envelope to the setting each day.

6. Give the envelopes to each of the children in turn. Help them to place the pieces and gradually build the puzzle and reveal the picture and cryptic message.

Question ideas

★ Who do you think is sending the puzzle pieces?

★ Why do you think someone would send us these puzzle pieces?

★ What do you think the message might say?

Taking it forward

- Provide the children with some blank jigsaw puzzles (available from www.amazon.co.uk) and felt pens so that they can create their own for each other to put together.

What's in it for the children?

This provocation aims to get children speculating as to where the puzzle is from and working together to solve it.

. . . .
Story suggestions

The Gruffalo Jigsaw Book by Julia Donaldson and Axel Scheffler (Macmillan)

The Selfish Crocodile by Faustin Charles and Michael Terry (Bloomsbury)
. . . .

Giant diorama

♥ Sensory provocation

What you need:

- Small room
- Sugar, tissue and crêpe paper in various shades of green, brown and yellow
- Green poster paper and display edging
- Kitchen paper rolls
- Green and brown string
- Camouflage netting
- Sticky tape, staple gun and staples
- Corrugated card
- Green and brown paint
- Pot plants – real and fake – in various sizes
- Hessian
- Green and brown fabric
- Straw
- Large rocks
- Leaves
- Jungle soundtrack (www.amazon.co.uk)

Question ideas

★ Where do you think you are?

★ What do you think you might find in a jungle?

★ What can you hear?

★ What do you think it might feel/ sound/smell like in a real jungle?

★ Can you move like a...?

What to do:

1. Transform a room in the setting into a giant jungle diorama:

   - line the floor with hessian and green and brown fabrics, and scatter leaves everywhere
   - place large rocks and potted plants all around
   - line display boards with green poster paper
   - hang camouflage netting from the ceiling and on the walls
   - paint corrugated card brown and use it to create tree trunks. Stick these on the walls and add paper leaves
   - make jungle vines by hanging strips of hessian from the ceiling and stapling leaves to them
   - link kitchen roll tubes together, paint them brown and add cardboard branches and leaves
   - play a jungle soundtrack in the background.

2. Allow the children space and time to play and explore.

Taking it forward

- Provide a jungle explorer kit: costume, rucksack, binoculars, camera, net.

- Provide animal costumes.

- Invite the children to make things and add them to the diorama.

- Challenge the children to create smaller dioramas in their own chosen themes, using large cardboard boxes and craft materials.

What's in it for the children?

This provocation encourages the children to imagine they are in a particular setting and conjure up language and vocabulary to describe their experience.

Story suggestions

Rumble in the Jungle by Giles Andreae and David Wojtowycz (Orchard)

Walking Through the Jungle by Julie Lacome (Walker)

Down in the Jungle by Elisa Squillace (Child's Play)

The new occupants

★ Fantastical provocation

What you need:

- Old dolls' house or large cardboard box and pieces of strong card
- Miniature furniture
- Objects that can be used as furniture: thimbles, building blocks, tiny plastic containers, cotton reels, buttons
- Felt, carpet offcuts, wallpaper samples
- Morsels of real food
- Miniature clothing
- Small battery operated lights

What to do:

1. Find an old dolls' house in a charity shop or car boot sale. Otherwise use a sturdy cardboard box and insert strong cardboard dividers.

2. Put the house somewhere out of the way but where the children can still see it. Gradually add things to the house:
   - line the floors with felt or offcuts of carpet
   - wallpaper the walls
   - add furniture to the rooms.

3. One morning, make the house look as though someone has moved in:
   - leave the front door open
   - add found objects, such as cotton reels for tables, thimbles for buckets and buttons for plates
   - half make the beds, as if they have been slept in
   - lay the table with a half-eaten breakfast using real food
   - fill the bath with warm soapy water
   - install some battery-operated lights and switch them on in the bathroom, bedroom and kitchen.

4. Wait for the children to realise that someone appears to have moved in.

Taking it forward

- Make it look as if the occupants have returned during the night. Move things around, change the food and switch different lights on. Continue to do this over the coming weeks.

- Invite the children to add furniture and decoration to the house.

What's in it for the children?

This provocation encourages children to jump into the world of make-believe and transfer this to their small world play.

Story suggestions

The Tale of Two Bad Mice by Beatrix Potter (Warne)

The Dolls' House Fairy by Jane Ray (Orchard)

Question ideas

★ What has happened here?

★ Who do you think has moved in?

★ Where do you think they have gone?

★ What do you think we should do?

The ringing telephone

✔ Problem-solving provocation

What you need:

- Brightly coloured telephone
- Working telephone line

What to do:

1. Plug a brightly coloured telephone into a working line and put it in a place that is easily accessible to the children.

2. Draw up a list of small challenges. For example:
   - make a repeating pattern
   - paint a flower
   - make a castle
   - collect five different types of leaf
   - make a pirate flag
   - build a bus.

3. Ask a member of staff to call the telephone periodically and reveal their identity before reading out a challenge.

4. Encourage the children to take turns answering the phone. After each call, help the child that answers relay the latest challenge to the other children.

5. Invite children to take on the role of the caller and assist them in phoning and delivering a challenge to their friends.

Taking it forward

- Provide old landline and mobile phones for the children to play with.

- Show children a variety of types of telephone from old ring dial phones to new smart phones with touch screens. Talk about how technology has changed.

What's in it for the children?

This provocation fosters communication and language skills. Children are required to listen to, process, relay and deliver instructions.

Story suggestions

Daddy's Day at Work, Grandad's Busy Day and Mummy's Big Day Out from the Fantastic Phones series by Greg Gormley (Bloomsbury)

Question ideas

★ Do you know how to use a telephone?

★ How do you greet someone when answering the phone?

★ Do you know who to call in na emergency? What number would you dial?

★ Do you know how to dial the number?

★ Can you think of a good idea for a challenge?

★ What are you going to say when they answer?

Musical mystery
★ Fantastical provocation

What you need:

- Mini MP3 players or dictaphones
- Selection of music in different genres

Taking it forward

- As the children discover the secret, invite them to choose more music to upload and hide in different areas. Help them to think about how different music makes them feel and why various genres can enhance learning and play in different areas of the setting.

What's in it for the children?

This provocation promotes children's listening skills. It encourages them to think about how music makes them feel and invites them to share their opinions with others.

Story suggestions

Can You Hear It? (with CD) by William Lach (Harry N. Abrams Inc)

My First Classical Music Book (with CD) by Genevieve Helsby and Jason Chapman (Naxos Books)

What's That Noise, Little Mouse? by Stephanie Stansbie and Polona Lovsin (Little Tiger Press)

What to do:

1. How you set up this provocation will depend upon how many MP3 players you have.

   Either: Hide a few MP3 players around the setting indoors and outside. Upload a different genre of music on each player and set it at a volume low enough that the children have to strain to hear it and will be confused as to where it is coming from.

   Or: Hide just one MP3 player in a different place each day and change the music each time.

2. Wait for the children to notice the music and let them deliberate as to where it is coming from and who put it there.

Question ideas

- ★ What can you hear?
- ★ What kind of music is that?
- ★ Who do you think is playing the music?
- ★ Why do you think they put it there?
- ★ How does that music make you feel?
- ★ Do you like that kind of music?

Wolf proof

✔ Problem-solving provocation

What you need:

- Paper
- Straw
- PVA glue
- Sticks (lollipop sticks are good)
- String
- Small red bricks
- Cement
- Sand
- Child-sized protective goggles
- Child-sized face masks
- Child-sized protective gloves
- Small cement trowels

Taking it forward

- See if the children can offer any suggestions for other building materials that they could use to build a stronger wall.
- Provide the children with puppets so that they can act out the story (uk.thepuppetcompany.com).

What's in it for the children?

This provocation prompts children to ask questions, test ideas and look for alternatives.

Story suggestions

The Three Pigs by David Wiesner (Andersen)

The True Story of the Three Little Pigs by Jon Scieszka and Lane Smith (Picture Puffin)

This is the House that Jack Built by Simms Taback (Puffin)

✚ Health & Safety

- Ensure children do not breathe in cement powder. Mix it away from them or give them protective goggles and masks to wear.
- Cement can irritate sensitive skin. Some children may need to wear protective gloves when using it.

What to do:

1. Prepare a letter from a little pig asking for advice about building a house that will be fully wolf–proof.
2. Post the letter to the setting.
3. Provide the children with samples of the various building materials used in the story – straw, sticks and bricks.
4. Assist the children in an investigation into which materials build the strongest wall or miniature house. Let them guide the investigation. Help them develop their ideas by providing resources and help.

Question ideas

★ How do you think we can make the sticks/straw/bricks stick together?

★ What do you think we could use?

★ How do you think we can make it stronger?

★ Which do you think is the strongest material?

★ How does it feel?

★ Is it possible to make bricks out of straw/sticks?

★ What happens if you make the wall taller/wider?

Invisible ink
★ Fantastical provocation

What you need:

- Blank white paper
- Pen
- Lemon
- Water
- Bowl and spoon
- Cotton buds
- Lamp

Taking it forward

- Provide the resources needed for the children to write their own invisible messages.

- Provide the children with a range of substances that they can experiment with to see if they are suitable for making invisible ink. Give them substances that will not work, for example, flour, soap and PVA glue, and some that will, such as vinegar, orange juice and milk.

What's in it for the children?

This provocation aims to get the children investigating and testing ideas to find out how something works.

Story suggestions

The Love Bugs by Simon Puttock and Russell Ayto (HarperCollins)

Health & Safety

Ensure children are supervised with lamps and exposed light bulbs, as they can get extremely hot.

What to do:

1. Set up a lamp somewhere in the setting that is very noticeable to the children.

2. Make some invisible ink by squeezing the juice of half a lemon into a bowl and mixing it with a few drops of water.

3. At the top of the piece of paper use a normal pen to write a riddle, such as: 'Things are not as they seem and need a light bulb to be seen.'

4. Dip a cotton bud into the lemon mixture and use it to write an invisible message underneath. There are various options and the message could be:

   - a greeting from a mystery pen pal followed up by invisible letters arriving in the post

   - a poem or rhyme

   - a picture

   - a single word that starts a sentence. The other words could be written on further pieces of paper and pegged around the setting for children to collect, reveal and arrange to construct the message.

5. Bring the invisible message to the children's attention one morning. Tell them you have no idea where it came from and ask them to help you solve the riddle written at the top.

6. Help the children to uncover the hidden message by holding the paper up in front of a lamp. The lemon juice will oxidise and turn brown under the heat of the bulb to reveal the message.

Question ideas

★ What do you think this riddle means?

★ What do you think we need to do?

★ Who do you think might have sent this message?

★ What kind of ink do you think the writer used?

★ What do you think the invisible ink is made out of?

Missing tooth

★ Fantastical provocation

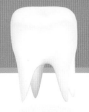

What you need:

- Glitter
- Fifty pence piece
- Large animal tooth

Or

- Clay or salt dough
- White paint

What to do:

1. Either use a large animal tooth or make a fake tooth out of clay or salt dough and paint it white. The tooth can be any size or shape and should look like it came from any type of animal.

2. Leave the tooth on a windowsill with a fifty pence piece lying next to it and sprinkle glitter all around.

Question ideas

★ What do you think it is?

★ Where do you think it came from?

★ What/who do you think left it there?

★ What do you think we should do about it?

Taking it forward

- Put the tooth somewhere safe over night. Sprinkle glitter around the setting leading into cupboards and around shelves to make it look as though something returned in the night to search for their lost property.

- Help the children think of ways to attract fairies into the setting.

What's in it for the children?

This provocation aims to rouse a sense of wonder within children and prompt them to build imaginative storylines.

Story suggestions

Freddie and the Fairy by Julia Donaldson and Karen George (Macmillan)

Lettice: The Fairy Ball by Mandy Stanley (HarperCollins)

The Complete Book of the Flower Fairies by Cicely Mary Baker (Warne)

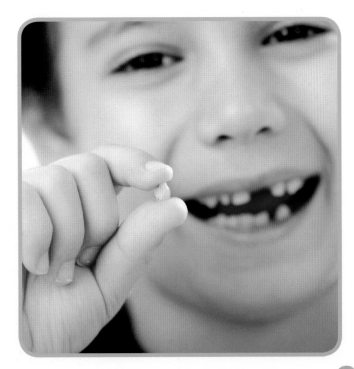

Round and round
♥ Sensory provocation

What you need:

- Selection of wheels: real, toy, large, small, wide, narrow, cogwheels, steering wheels
- Things that can be used as ramps: pieces of wood, cardboard tubes, very large bowls
- Selection of wheeled toys: small vehicles, pull-along toys, ride-on vehicles, gears construction kit
- Video of a Catherine wheel firework in action
- Laptop and projector

Taking it forward

- Challenge the children to experiment with using different shapes to make wheels.
- Encourage the children to move objects around using rollers and planks of wood.

What's in it for the children?

This provocation aims to get children investigating and experimenting with size, shape, movement and force.

Story suggestions

Bears on Wheels by Stan and Jan Berenstain (Random House)

Best Friend on Wheels by Debra Shirley and Judy Stead (Albert Whitman & Company)

Pete the Cat: The Wheels on the Bus by James Dean (HarperCollins)

What to do:

1. Cover the setting in all kinds of wheels:
   - place individual wheels everywhere for the children to examine and play with
   - set out a range of objects that can be used to make ramps
   - project a video of a Catherine wheel whizzing around on the wall
   - provide a selection of wheeled toys.

2. When the children arrive, give them time and space to play with the wheels and toys.

3. Follow the children's lead and provide assistance and support for any investigations or activities they embark upon.

Question ideas

★ What do you think that wheel is used for?

★ Where do you think that wheel comes from?

★ What do you think would happen if …?

★ Have you ever seen a wheel like that before?

★ How do you think that works?

50 fantastic ideas for imaginative thinking

Bringing in the bees

✔ Problem-solving provocation

What you need:

- **Information book about bees** (some age appropriate books include *Bees & Wasps* by James Maclaine and John Francis (Usborne Beginners) and *Are You a Bee?* by Judy Allen and Tudor Humphries (Kingfisher))
- **Flower seeds**
- **Flowering plants**
- **Child-sized gardening tools**

Taking it forward

- Provide magnifying glasses for the children to closely observe the bees that visit. Help the children take photographs to create a display about what bees do.
- Take the children to visit a beekeeper to find out how honey is produced and harvested. Taste honey.

What's in it for the children?

This provocation teaches children how to gather information and use what they learn to organise, plan and execute a project.

> **Story suggestions**
>
> *The Very Greedy Bee* by Steve Smallman and Jack Tickle (Little Tiger Press)
>
> *Bee-Wigged* by Cece Bell (Walker)
>
> *The Bear and the Bees* by Ella Richardson and Lydia Monks (Macmillan)

What to do:

1. Help the children learn about the importance of bees. Use the internet and information books to teach the children about the difference between bumble bees and honey bees. Find out about how bees pollinate plants. Explain that these important minibeasts are becoming less common.

2. If possible, go outside and look for bees. Observe them flying between flowers, transferring pollen and collecting nectar.

3. Ask the children for some ideas about how they could attract bees to the outdoor area of their setting.

4. Help the children put their ideas into action; plant flowers that will attract bees.

Question ideas

★ What do bees like?

★ What do you think we need to do to make them want to come here?

★ Where do you think we could go to get what we need?

★ What type of bee is that? How do you know?

★ Why are bees so important?

A matter of taste
♥ Sensory provocation

What you need:

- Home-made apple and rhubarb crumble
- Ingredients to make another apple and rhubarb crumble
- Extra ingredients: bread, salt, pears, sultanas, nutmeg

What to do:

1. Make an apple and rhubarb crumble:

FOOD allergy !

Ingredients

200g rhubarb

150g cooking apples

sugar to sweeten

water

1tsp cinnamon

50g margarine

100g self raising flour

50g caster sugar

Method

1   Chop the rhubarb and apples into small pieces and stew in a pan with a splash of water and sugar to sweeten. Add some cinnamon.

2.   Rub the margarine, flour and caster sugar together until the mixture resembles breadcrumbs.

3.   Pour the fruit mixture into an ovenproof dish and scatter the crumble over the top.

4.   Bake at 190°C / gas mark 5 for 30 minutes.

2. Work with the children in small groups:

- show them the ready-made crumble
- show them the ingredients – both actual and additional
- share out some portions of crumble for the children to look at, taste and smell
- do the same with the raw ingredients
- ask the children if they can pick out which ingredients were used to make this particular crumble.

50 fantastic ideas for imaginative thinking

Question ideas

★ What ingredients can you see in the crumble?

★ What ingredients can you taste?

★ Do you know what I used to make this crumble?

★ Have you ever cooked a crumble before?

★ Do you like apples/rhubarb/cinnamon?

✚ Health & Safety

- If you allow the children to taste raw rhubarb, bear in mind that rhubarb leaves are poisonous.

- Take care to ensure no one is allergic or intolerant to any of the ingredients in this recipe.

Taking it forward

■ Ask the children to suggest alternative crumble ingredients and help them to make crumbles of their own.

■ Play blindfold games with a variety of foods and get children using their senses of taste, touch and smell to identify them.

What's in it for the children?

This provocation involves children using their senses to examine and identify foods. It also encourages them to express their likes and dislikes.

Story suggestions

Pancake Pandemonium by Anita Pouroulis and Tom Bonson (Digital Leaf)

Delicious! by Helen Cooper (Picture Corgi)

Gingerbread crumbs

★ Fantastical provocation

What you need:

- **Ingredients to make gingerbread people** (Find a good recipe in *Be-Ro Flour Home Recipes 40th Edition* (The Be-Ro Kitchen))
- Oven
- Baking tray
- Greaseproof paper

FOOD allergy!

Taking it forward

- Encourage the children to draw on their knowledge of traditional tales. Can they tell you the story of the Gingerbread Man?
- Provide the children with puppets so that they can act out the story (uk.thepuppetcompany.com).

What's in it for the children?

This provocation asks children to recall their knowledge of a story and draw on this to formulate ideas and explanations.

Story suggestions

The Gingerbread Man by Estelle Corke (Child's Play)

Gingerbread Baby by Jan Brett (Putnam Publishing)

Ten Gingerbread Men by Ruth Galloway (Caterpillar Books)

✚ Health & Safety

Ensure the oven is fully cooled before allowing the children to enter the kitchen area. Be aware of any food allergies and intolerances if the children are eating the gingerbread men.

What to do:

1. Make gingerbread people with the children. Ensure you make an extra gingerbread of your own. Time the activity so that the gingerbread is in the oven over lunchtime or before the children go outside for another activity.

2. Bake the gingerbread people.

3. Take them out of the oven and leave the oven door open to cool. Crumble the extra gingerbread person that you made to make crumbs. Scatter the crumbs along the open oven door, across the floor and leading out of the kitchen area.

4. Hide the rest of the gingerbread people around the setting.

5. Bring the children back into the kitchen and pretend to be surprised.

Question ideas

★ What do you think has happened?

★ Where have they gone?

★ What can you see?

★ Why do you think they have run away?

★ Can you think of any stories where this has happened before?

Stranded

✔ Problem-solving provocation

What you need:

- Paddling pool
- Junk: cardboard and plastic food containers, lolly sticks, corks, yoghurt pots, egg boxes
- Cling film, card, paper and cellophane
- Glue and sticky tape
- String and scissors
- Large rock
- Small toy character

What to do:

1. Fill a paddling pool with water and place a large rock in the centre.
2. Put a small toy character on the rock.
3. Challenge the children to build a boat that is strong enough to carry the toy character to safety without sinking.
4. Guide the children. Help them to test out various materials and choose which are best suited to boat building.

Question ideas

★ Which materials do you think will float?

★ Which materials do you think are strong enough to hold the toy?

★ How do you plan to stick it together?

★ Why have you chosen to use that?

★ What do you think will happen if that gets wet?

★ What are you going to use that for?

★ Is there anything else that you might need?

Taking it forward

- Bring the children together to test out each boat. Ask the children to consider why some float and others do not.
- Talk about water safety. Ask the children what they would do in a real life situation like this.
- Find out about the Royal National Lifeboat Institution (www.rnli.org).

What's in it for the children?

This provocation involves testing out materials to decide which are best suited for a particular purpose. Children are challenged to come up with a creative design and build a model that works.

Story suggestions

Busy Boats by Tony Mitton and Ant Parker (Kingfisher)

Mr Grumpy's Outing by John Burningham (Red Fox)

All Afloat on Noah's Boat by Tony Mitton and Guy Parker-Rees (Orchard)

✚ Health & Safety

Ensure the children are supervised at all times when playing and working around the paddling pool.

A safe passage
✔ Problem-solving provocation

What you need:

- Large space – indoors or outside
- Selection of climbing equipment: bench, stepping stones, pop-up tunnel, slide, wooden blocks
- Toy bear
- Paper and pen
- Additional adults to help move large equipment

⊕ Health & Safety
Ensure there are a sufficient number of adults to assist in lifting and moving heavy equipment.

What to do:

1. Put a toy bear at the far end of a large open space.

2. Gather together a selection of climbing equipment and place it at the opposite end of the space.

3. Set out the challenge on a piece of paper and place it with the equipment. For example:

   'Little Bear has found himself stuck on the other side of a magical swamp. Set one foot on the floor and you too will be stuck! Your challenge is to rescue Little Bear and bring him safely back.'

4. Obviously the children will need to walk on the 'swamp' during the challenge to place the equipment. So include an additional note explaining that they must shout 'FREEZE' before they do so. Explain that this will momentarily 'harden' the floor while they build their path across. However, this magic will no longer work during the rescue.

5. Bring the children to the challenge in small groups. Read out the sheet and ask them for their ideas and suggestions about how to rescue Little Bear. Help them to consider and evaluate the merits of each other's suggestions.

6. Allow the children to direct you as you assist in placing the equipment where they want it and create a path to the bear.

Question ideas

★ What do you think you need to do?

★ Why do/don't you think that is a good idea?

★ How can you check if that is safe?

★ What do you think might happen if you put that there?

★ What else do you need?

Taking it forward

■ Ask the children to consider how safe it is to carry the bear back in their hands while navigating climbing equipment. Can they think of a safer way to transport the bear? Is there anything they can use to help?

What's in it for the children?

This provocation involves the children in working together to form strategies and evaluate ideas before coming up with a viable solution.

Story suggestions

We're Going on a Bear Hunt by Michael Rosen and Helen Oxenbury (Walker)

In the dark
♥ Sensory provocation

What you need:

- Large open space in a room that can easily be darkened
- Black sugar paper
- Large objects: slide, chair, tricycle, sturdy clothes horse, giant cuddly toy
- Fibre optic fountains

Taking it forward

- Provide torches for the children to explore the room for a second time and look at the objects using torchlight.
- Use eye masks for a scaled down version of this activity. Place small objects on a table or inside a feely bag for children to examine with their hands and guess what they are.

What's in it for the children?

This provocation requires children to use their senses to compensate for the absence of sight. It encourages them to think of language to describe what they can feel and use the clues to come to a logical conclusion.

> **Story suggestions**
>
> *Mog in the Dark* by Judith Kerr (HarperCollins)
>
> *Darkness Slipped In* by Ella Burfoot (Kingfisher)
>
> *The Dark* by Lemony Snicket and Jon Klassen (Orchard)

➕ **Health & Safety**

Only take a small number of children into the dark room at a time to avoid collisions. Ensure there are enough adults available to guide the children as they move around the obstacles.

What to do:

1. Darken a large room by sticking black sugar paper over windows and closing curtains.

2. Place a number of large everyday objects around the room. Leave space for the children to safely walk in between and around the objects.

3. Place a fibre optic fountain in each corner of the room. These will emit a small amount of light for safety.

4. Bring the children into the room in small groups. Guide them around the room to find the objects, feel them and guess what they are.

Question ideas

★ What can you see?

★ What does it feel like?

★ Can you describe the shape?

★ What do you think it is made out of?

★ What do you think it is?

Dream balloons

★ Fantastical provocation

What you need:

- Shiny, sparkly balloons
- Silver or gold string
- Glitter
- Funnel
- Small pieces of coloured paper
- Pen

Taking it forward

- Provide art materials for children to draw and paint pictures of the dreams they discover, as well as their own dreams.

- Ask the children if they can make up some dream sequences. Encourage them to think of unusual ideas, including strange happenings and events that do not make sense.

What's in it for the children?

This provocation helps children to process and make sense of dreams. It also prompts them to come up with imaginative and fantastical ideas of their own.

Story suggestions

The Book of Dreams by Shirin Adl (Frances Lincoln)

Arthur's Dream Boat by Polly Dunbar (Walker)

The Beasties by Jenny Nimmo and Gwen Millward (Egmont)

✚ Health & Safety

Some children are very sensitive to the sound of balloons popping, particularly those with special educational needs. Take care that the children don't inhale any pieces of popped balloon.

What to do:

1. Take some small pieces of coloured paper (about 15 or so) and write strange dream sequences on them. Include scary dreams as well as fun ones. For example:

   - Flying above the clouds with pterodactyls.

   - Jumping on a bed of marshmallow and sticking to the ceiling.

   - Being chased by monsters and hiding under the bed.

   - Riding on a steam train between mountains, through tunnels and over bridges.

   - Standing on the moon and fishing for stars with nets.

   - Dancing with fairies on a stage.

   - Getting lost in a forest.

   - Sitting upside down on a bus going nowhere.

2. Fold or roll up each piece of paper so that it is small enough to fit through the neck of a balloon.

3. Put the dreams inside the balloons, use a funnel to add some glitter and blow the balloons up.

4. Use string to attach the balloons to various cuddly toys and characters around the setting. You could even attach balloons to some practitioners.

5. When the children arrive, allow them to play with the balloons and discover that there is something inside. Let the children pop the balloons if they choose. Read the dream sequences out and let the children decide what they mean.

Question ideas

- ★ What do you think is inside?

- ★ What do you think it means?

- ★ What did you dream about last night?

- ★ Do you ever have bad dreams?

- ★ Why do you think we have dreams?

50 fantastic ideas for imaginative thinking

Get organised

✔ Problem-solving provocation

What you need:

- Labels and pens
- Trollies with stacked baskets
- Storage boxes
- Baskets
- Tubs

Taking it forward

- Divide the children into working parties and make each child responsible for a particular area. Draw up a pictorial jobs rota to remind the children to keep their area tidy and point out to adults when things need replenishing.

- Periodically ask the children if they are happy with the organisation and if they can suggest any ideas for further improvement.

What's in it for the children?

This provocation encourages the children to think of practical solutions and requires them to work together to put ideas into action. It also presents opportunity for later reflection and reevaluation.

> **Story suggestions**
>
> *Tidy Titch* by Pat Hutchins (Red Fox)
>
> *Little Miss Tidy* by Roger Hargreaves (Egmont)

What to do:

1. Present the children with a problem. Explain that the toys and resources in the setting are constantly getting mixed up, lost and broken. Ask if any of the children can suggest any solutions.

2. Draw a mind map of the children's ideas and suggestions.

3. Ask them to explain how they think you could put the ideas into action.

4. Challenge the children to help reorganise the toys and resources around the setting.

Question ideas

★ Where do you think is the best place to keep this?

★ Will it be easy to reach if we put it there?

★ How will everyone know where it is kept?

★ What might happen if we leave this here?

Lost luggage

★ Fantastical provocation

What you need:

- Suitcase
- Personal luggage label
- Airline barcoded luggage label (*make your own imitation*)
- Personal items that give clues as to the owner and their intended destination
- Travel brochures
- Globe or world map

What to do:

1. Pack a suitcase with personal items. Decide where the intended destination is and pack accordingly. For example, summer clothing, sunglasses and sun cream for a beach holiday and winter woollies, hats and scarves for a skiing holiday.

2. Write a personal luggage label with a name and address. Rip the label and smudge the writing with water so it is difficult to read the details.

3. Create an airline luggage label with a flight number and barcode.

4. Ask someone to deliver the suitcase to the setting, explaining that they are unable to trace the owner.

Question ideas

★ How do you think we can find out who the case belongs to?

★ What kind of holiday might you wear these clothes on?

★ Who do you think might wear clothes like this?

★ What country do you think they might be travelling to?

★ How do you think you think the owner was planning on getting there?

★ Have you ever been abroad on a plane or boat?

★ What do you think we should do next?

Taking it forward

- Look through travel brochures at different types of holiday and help the children decide where the luggage is destined. Use a globe or world map to help them figure out what mode of transport the holiday maker would need to get there.

- Help the children decide what to do with the case.

What's in it for the children?

This provocation asks children to look at evidence, make connections and come up reasoned explanations.

> **Story suggestions**
>
> *Maisy Goes on Holiday* by Lucy Cousins (Walker)

Art studio
♥ Sensory provocation

What you need:

- Various types of paper: sugar, cartridge, papyrus, crêpe, tissue
- PVA, glue sticks, scissors, stencils, sticky tape, staplers, hole punches
- Crafty bits and pieces: feathers, buttons, spangles, lollipop sticks, coloured sand, foam shapes, stickers, ribbon, wooden shavings, fabric cuttings, junk
- Selection of coloured and metallic paints: poster, watercolour
- Paint brushes, rollers, printing sponges, pallets
- Coloured pencils, chalks, crayons, felt pens, pastels
- Natural objects: leaves, pinecones, shells, twigs, seeds, dried flowers, dried pulses
- Easels, light boxes and overhead projectors
- Objects to display that will capture the children's imaginations, including found, natural and everyday objects and pictures

What to do:

1. Transform the setting into an art studio:

- put out the art resources listed above (and anything else that you can think of) in trays and tubs around the setting
- set up easels
- arrange the tables so that the children have a variety of different sized work surfaces to use
- clear a large area of floor space for the children to use
- place objects and pictures around the setting for the children to look at and explore
- set up a light box and overhead projector with items to experiment with alongside.

2. Allow the children time and space to explore the resources and create.

Question ideas

★ What can you see?
★ Can you describe that for me?
★ What would you like to make/draw/paint?
★ Is there anything else you need?
★ Can you tell me about what you have done?
★ How does that make you feel?
★ Why have you decided to do that?

Health & Safety
Ensure children are supervised with scissors and staplers, as well as the overhead projector if it has an exposed light bulb, as it can get extremely hot.

Taking it forward

- Observe the children and look for their preoccupations. Provide resources that will foster these interests.

- Invite the children to bring more resources in from home.

- Invite parents in to spend time creating artwork with their children.

- Ask children to choose music to play in the background.

What's in it for the children?

This provocation invites children to find original ways to represent their ideas, thoughts and feelings using a range of artistic methods.

Story suggestions

I absolutely MUST do colouring now or painting or drawing and *I completely MUST do drawing now and painting and colouring*, both by Lauren Child (Grosset & Dunlap)

The Magic Paintbrush by Julia Donaldson and Joel Stewart (Igloo/Macmillan)

50 fantastic ideas for imaginative thinking

What next?

✔ Problem-solving provocation

What you need:

- Large character puppets or cuddly toys
- Digital camera
- Laptop and projector

Taking it forward

- Use such photographs to prompt discussion whenever an issue arises that needs to be addressed. For instance, when children are running indoors or jumping off the climbing frame.

What's in it for the children?

This provocation helps children to evaluate risk, predict outcomes and consider consequences.

What to do:

1. Take a large character puppet or soft toy out and take photographs of it in various precarious situations. For example:
   - climbing a tree
   - balancing on a wall
   - standing at the edge of a pond
   - climbing on some scaffolding
   - playing with a football at the side of a road
   - swinging on a gate.

2. Take a second set of photographs of possible outcomes. For example:
   - on the floor at the foot of the tree
   - on the floor at the foot of the wall
   - in the pond
   - lying on the scaffold with a brick on his leg
   - next to the football in the road with cars driving towards it
   - trapped under the gate.

3. Bring the children together to show them the photographs. Start with a photograph from the first set. Ask the children to explain what is happening in the picture and to consider what might happen next.

Question ideas

★ What is happening in the picture?

★ Why do you think he is doing that?

★ What do you think might happen next?

★ How do you think she feels?

★ Do you think that is a good idea? Why/why not?

★ Can you think of a safer place to climb/balance/run/play?

Story suggestions

The Tale of Peter Rabbit by Beatrix Potter (Warne)

The Further Tale of Peter Rabbit by Emma Thompson and Eleanor Taylor (Warne)

50 fantastic ideas for imaginative thinking

Mystery mail
★ Fantastical provocation

What you need:

- Very large envelope
- Large piece of paper
- Black and red felt pens
- Coloured paper
- Glue
- Empty boxes and brown parcel paper
- Brown and white envelopes
- Fake postage stamps (available from www.twinkl.co.uk)

Question ideas

- ★ Who do you think would send a letter like this?
- ★ What makes you think that?
- ★ Do you think we should open it and read it? Why/why not?
- ★ What do you think we should do?

Taking it forward

- Introduce more 'lost' letters in various sizes, colours and shapes. Put clues in each of the letters for the children to guess the identities of the senders.
- Help the children to create their own mystery mail.

What's in it for the children?

This provocation involves children listening closely for details and clues, making links and drawing conclusions.

Story suggestions

The Jolly Postman by Janet and Allan Ahlberg (Puffin)

Meerkat Mail by Emily Gravett (Macmillan)

What to do:

1. Write a letter on a very large piece of paper, as if a giant may have written it. The letter can be about anything, but should include some clues as to who has sent it (see the example below).

2. Seal the letter in a very large envelope. Make a giant-sized stamp using some coloured paper and stick it on. Draw a postmark over the stamp and write on an imaginary address.

Claudia Grossbottom
18 Grunge Drive
Enormaton Way
Fairy Land, FL42 7FQ

1 Green Bean Avenue
Cloud Bank
Fairy Land
FL63 8GB

Dearest Claudia

I hope you are well. How was your holiday in the Lakes? I hope you didn't eat too much Kendal mint cake!

It has been two weeks since the boy ran away and left me to fend for myself without so much as a golden nugget to buy myself some bread and cheese. I have been watching the bottom of the garden in case he reappears and live in the hope that he might feel sorry for me and bring my goose back.

Lucinda says to tell you thank you for the bucket of raspberry jam. It has certainly helped to get us through this difficult time.

We look forward to seeing you again in the summer.

Lots of love from, Hubert xxx

3. Draw a big red stamp on the front of the envelope saying 'LOST MAIL'.

4. Set up a role-play post office with sorting office. Fill it with mundane looking post, for example, parcels wrapped in brown paper and average sized letters in white and brown envelopes.

5. After the children have spent time playing in the post office for a few days, put the unusual looking giant letter on the counter for them to find.

The Riddler

✔ Problem-solving provocation

What you need:

- Envelopes
- Paper
- Fake postage stamps

Taking it forward

- Help the children to create their own riddles. Send the riddles back to the Riddler for him/her to solve.
- Ask parents to help their children make up riddles at home to bring into the setting.

What's in it for the children?

This provocation involves children drawing on their own knowledge and listening closely for details and clues to solve puzzles.

> **Story suggestions**
>
> *Sir Charlie Stinky Socks and the Tale of the Two Treasures* by Kristina Stephenson (Egmont)
>
> *Katie Morag and the Riddles* by Mairi Hedderwick (Red Fox)

What to do:

1. Make up some riddles that the children will be able to solve. For example:

Who am I?

I have long golden hair
and a nose for a tasty breakfast;
I like a comfortable chair
and I can run very fast.

What are we?

Mix us until we are light and fluffy
and bake us until we rise;
Give us hats that are sweet and sugary
and hide us from the flies.

What am I?

I have two pointy ears
and like climbing up trees;
I have a long furry tail
and like warm comfy knees.

2. Write the riddles on pieces of paper and sign them off 'The Riddler'. Seal them in envelopes and address them to the setting. Put on a fake stamp and draw on a fake postmark.

3. Arrange it so that one riddle arrives at the setting each morning for a week.

Question ideas

★ Where do you think this has come from?

★ What do you think we need to do?

★ What do you think this means?

★ Can you solve the riddle?

Box of tricks

♥ Sensory provocation

What you need:

- **Rainbow talking boxes** (available from www.spacekraft.co.uk)
- **Shredded crêpe paper**
- **Selection of small everyday objects**
- **Dry wipe marker pens**
- **Blindfolds**

What to do:

1. Put an object in each box and cover it with shredded crêpe paper.

2. Record a ten second sound message that offers clues as to what is in the box. For example:
   - **Pine cone** – It is brown and fell off a tree
   - **Toy car** – It has four wheels but cannot drive on its own
   - **Spoon** – It is made of metal and is used to scoop liquid from a bowl
   - **Gloves** – These keep your fingers warm in the snow
   - **Chalk** – Use this to draw with and wipe away

3. Pass the boxes around for the children to listen to the clues and guess what is hidden inside. Allow the children to feel the objects blindfolded or with their eyes closed.

4. Use a dry wipe pen to record the children's names along with their guesses on the lid of each box.

5. Reveal the contents and see who was right.

Question ideas

★ What do you think the clue is hinting at?

★ Can you describe what the object feels like?

★ Do you still think the same or have you changed your mind?

★ Do you agree with the other guesses? Why/why not?

Taking it forward

- Ask the children to choose objects to hide in the boxes. Help them to think of simple descriptive clues and make their own recordings.

- Use a feely bag and a tape recorder to do the same activity.

What's in it for the children?

This provocation requires children to use their senses of hearing and touch to gather information and make connections.

Story suggestions

Read books that encourage children to listen to the details in descriptive clues including:

Spot's Treasure Hunt by Eric Hill (Puffin)

Monkey Puzzle by Julia Donaldson and Axel Scheffler (Macmillan)

50 fantastic ideas for imaginative thinking

Surveillance shot

★ Fantastical provocation

What you need:

- Popular and familiar cuddly toys or puppets from the setting
- Digital camera
- Laptop and projector

What to do:

1. Take surveillance photos of a large character puppet or soft toy engaged in everyday tasks. For example:
   - shopping at the supermarket
   - playing at the park
   - feeding the ducks
   - eating at a restaurant
   - exercising at the gym
   - driving a car.

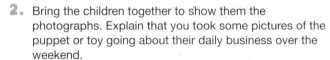

2. Bring the children together to show them the photographs. Explain that you took some pictures of the puppet or toy going about their daily business over the weekend.

3. Ask the children to explain what the puppet is doing in the photograph. Encourage them to share their own experiences of such activities.

Question ideas

★ What is she doing?

★ Have you ever done that?

★ Have you ever been there before?

★ Why do you think she is doing that?

★ Where do you think she is going?

Taking it forward

- Send home digital or disposable cameras for the children to take photographs of the every day activities they engage in. Help them upload their photographs to create slide shows. Encourage them to explain to their friends what they are doing in the photographs.

What's in it for the children?

This provocation encourages children to communicate what they can see and relate it to their own experiences.

> **Story suggestions**
>
> *Having a Picnic, Going Shopping, Doing the Washing* and *Going Swimming* all by Sarah Garland (Frances Lincoln)

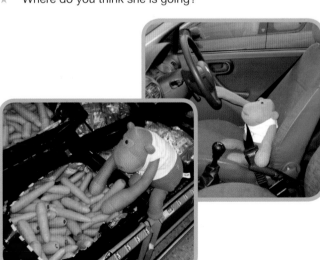